Setting your Financial Goals

Wealth Strategies

Setting your Financial Goals

Wealth Strategies

The roadmap to financial freedom

Richard Green

Cover design by Ropdi Designs
Cover background and internal page opener images by Ropdi Designs
Internal design and figures by Pixel Inspirations

Disclaimer

The content in this publication is a form of general commentary and should not be construed as professional advice. It is not meant to offer specific guidance for individual situations, and individuals should not depend on it as the sole basis for making decisions to take or abstain from any actions discussed within. Before making any such decisions, readers are advised to seek professional guidance where appropriate. The author disclaims all responsibility and liability, to the fullest extent permitted by law, for any consequences arising directly or indirectly from individuals taking or refraining from action based on the information provided in this publication. Please note that this publication may not contain the most current information available.

Contents

Acknowledgements

I extend my deepest gratitude to my father for his profound wisdom that has guided the creation of "Setting Your Financial Goals: Wealth Strategies".

To my mentors, advisors, family, and friends, your unwavering support has been instrumental in this journey.

And to the readers, may this book inspire and empower you on your path to financial success.

Thank you all for being part of this incredible voyage.in my abilities have fuelled my determination and propelled me toward success.

About the author

Richard Green is a seasoned financial expert and entrepreneur dedicated to empowering individuals on their journey to financial success. With a wealth of experience in entrepreneurship, investing, and personal finance, Richi has spent years studying and mastering the principles of wealth creation and abundance.

Drawing inspiration from luminaries and mentors, Richi has distilled their knowledge and insights into a comprehensive guide that offers practical strategies and actionable advice for achieving seven-figure wealth. Through their writing, Richi seeks to inspire and empower readers to take control of their financial destiny, guiding them along the path to prosperity with wisdom, clarity, and unwavering determination.

With a passion for helping others achieve their financial goals, Richi brings a unique blend of expertise, empathy, and enthusiasm to his work. Whether through books, seminars, or one-on-one coaching, Richi is committed to sharing his knowledge and insights to help individuals unlock their full potential and create a life of abundance and fulfilment.

"Elevate your wealth, elevate society"

How to use this book

In this book, we've condensed decades of financial wisdom into actionable steps designed to empower you on your journey to financial independence. To make the most of this resource, let's explore how you can effectively utilize its contents:

Start with an Open Mind
Approach this book with an open mind and a willingness to challenge your existing beliefs about money and wealth. Embrace the opportunity to learn new concepts and strategies that can transform your financial future.

Engage in Active Reading
As you read each chapter, engage actively with the material. Take notes, highlight key points, and reflect on how the concepts discussed apply to your own financial situation. Consider journaling your thoughts and insights to deepen your understanding.

Apply What You Learn
Knowledge without action is merely potential. Throughout the book, you'll encounter practical exercises and action steps designed to help you apply the principles discussed. Don't just read passively - take action and implement the strategies outlined to see real results in your financial life.

Customize Your Approach
Recognize that everyone's financial journey is unique. While the strategies presented in this book provide a solid foundation for success, feel free to adapt and customize them to suit your individual goals, values, and circumstances.

Stay Committed and Persistent

Building wealth is a journey that requires commitment and persistence. Expect challenges and setbacks along the way but remain steadfast in your determination to achieve your financial goals. Remember, every step forward, no matter how small, brings you closer to your desired destination.

Seek Support and Accountability

Don't hesitate to seek support and accountability as you work towards your financial goals. Share your aspirations with trusted friends, family members, or mentors who can offer encouragement, guidance, and accountability along the way.

Review and Reflect Regularly

Periodically review your progress and reflect on your financial goals and strategies. Celebrate your achievements, learn from your mistakes, and adjust your approach as needed to stay on track towards financial success.

Share Your Success Stories

As you experience success and achieve your financial goals, consider sharing your stories and insights with others. Pay it forward by inspiring and empowering those around you to take control of their financial futures and pursue their own dreams of wealth and abundance.

By following these guidelines and fully engaging with the material presented in "Setting Your Financial Goals: Wealth Strategies," you'll be well-equipped to embark on a transformative journey towards financial freedom and prosperity.

Remember, the power to shape your financial destiny lies in your hands. So, seize this opportunity, take action, and embark on the path to a brighter financial future today.

Chapter 1
Defining Your Vision:
What Does Financial Success
Mean to You?

Welcome to the journey of financial enlightenment, where we'll delve deep into the very foundation of your financial journey: defining your vision for success. In this chapter, we'll explore the fundamental question: What does financial success mean to you?

Understanding your personal vision of financial success is crucial. It serves as the guiding light, the North Star that will navigate you through the turbulent waters of wealth creation. To guide you on this introspective journey, I'll share insights and anecdotes from my own path to financial freedom.

Firstly, let's debunk a common myth: Financial success isn't merely about accumulating a vast sum of money. Sure, money is a critical component, but true financial success encompasses far more than just wealth. It's about achieving a state of abundance in all aspects of life: financial, emotional, and spiritual.

So, take a moment to reflect. What does financial success truly mean to you? Is it the freedom to travel the world without worrying about expenses? Is it the ability to provide for your loved ones, ensuring their comfort and security? Or perhaps it's the satisfaction of pursuing your passions without being enslaved by financial constraints?

For me, financial success isn't about flaunting opulent possessions or living a life of extravagance. It's about having the freedom to make choices without being shackled by monetary limitations. It's the ability to live life on my terms, to pursue my passions, and to contribute meaningfully to the world.

Your vision of financial success should be deeply personal and aligned with your core values. It's not about conforming to societal norms or chasing someone else's idea of success. It's about honouring your authentic self and crafting a life that resonates with your soul.

To help clarify your vision, consider the following questions:

What are your short-term and long-term financial goals?
How do you envision your ideal lifestyle?
What are your core values, and how do they influence your financial decisions?
What legacy do you want to leave behind for future generations?
How do you define financial freedom, and what steps are you willing to take to achieve it?

Once you've defined your vision of financial success, write it down and revisit it regularly. Let it serve as a beacon of inspiration, guiding you through the inevitable challenges and setbacks along your journey.

Remember, the path to financial success is not always smooth sailing. There will be obstacles, detours, and storms to weather. But with a clear vision and unwavering determination, you can navigate through any adversity and emerge stronger on the other side.

In the words of the great Warren Buffett, "Someone's sitting in the shade today because someone planted a tree a long time ago." So, plant the seeds of your financial vision today, and watch as they blossom into the abundant life you've always dreamed of.

Stay tuned for the next chapter, where we'll delve into assessing your current financial situation and laying the groundwork for your journey to financial freedom. Until then, keep dreaming big and taking bold actions towards your vision of success.

Chapter 2
Assessing Your Current Financial Situation

Welcome, financial voyager, to the second leg of our expedition toward wealth and freedom. The first step towards getting somewhere is to decide that you are not going to stay where you are." In this chapter, we're about to embark on a pivotal quest: assessing your current financial landscape.

Imagine your financial situation as a vast terrain, with hills and valleys, winding roads, and hidden treasures. Your task now is to survey this terrain with keen eyes, to map out its contours, and to understand where you stand in the grand scheme of wealth creation.

Let's begin this expedition with a thorough inventory of your financial assets and liabilities. Assemble all your financial documents, from bank statements and investment portfolios to mortgage agreements and credit card bills. These documents are your compass, guiding you through the labyrinth of your financial landscape.

Income Streams: Start by charting the streams of income flowing into your coffers. This might include your salary, bonuses, rental income, dividends, interest payments, or any other sources of revenue. Take note of the stability and consistency of each income stream, as well as its growth potential.

Expenses Expedition: Now, turn your attention to the outflows from your financial reservoir. Document every expense, from the essential (housing, utilities, groceries) to the discretionary (dining out, entertainment, vacations). Pay close attention to any recurring expenses that might be draining your resources unnecessarily.

Assets Archipelago: Cast your gaze across the archipelago of your assets. These might include cash reserves, investment accounts, retirement funds, real estate holdings, business interests, and valuable possessions. Consider the liquidity, growth potential, and diversification of each asset in your portfolio.

Liabilities Labyrinth: Next, venture into the labyrinth of your liabilities. These might include mortgages, car loans, student loans, credit card debts, personal loans, or any other financial obligations weighing on your shoulders. Calculate the total amount owed, as well as the interest rates and repayment terms for each liability.

As you traverse this financial terrain, take stock of your surroundings. Assess the health of your financial ecosystem with a critical eye, asking yourself probing questions:

Are your income streams robust and diversified, or are you overly reliant on a single source of revenue?
Are your expenses aligned with your priorities and values, or are they consuming more of your income than you'd like?
Are your assets growing steadily, or are they stagnant or depreciating in value?
Are your liabilities manageable, or are they threatening to engulf you in a sea of debt?

This expedition into your financial landscape is not merely an exercise in number-crunching; it's a journey of self-discovery and empowerment. As you confront the realities of your financial situation, you gain clarity, insight, and the courage to chart a new course toward prosperity.

In the next chapter, we'll harness the insights gleaned from this assessment to chart a course toward your financial destination. So, strap on your boots, tighten your backpack and prepare to traverse the rugged terrain of wealth creation.

The path ahead may be challenging, but with determination and foresight, you'll navigate it with grace and resilience.

Chapter 3
Identifying Short-Term and Long-Term Goals

Congratulations on embarking on this journey toward financial mastery! In this chapter, we'll delve deep into the crucial task of identifying both short-term and long-term financial goals. Goals give you a direction and purpose in life. They help you focus your energy and resources."

Short-Term Goals: Paving the Path to Progress

Short-term goals are the stepping stones that propel you forward on your journey to financial success. These goals typically have a timeline of one to three years and serve as the building blocks for achieving your long-term aspirations. When setting short-term goals, consider the following:

Debt Reduction: If you're burdened by high-interest debt, such as credit card balances or personal loans, prioritize paying off these debts to free up financial resources for other goals.

Emergency Fund: Establishing an emergency fund is essential to weather unexpected financial crises. Aim to save at least three to six months' worth of living expenses in a readily accessible account.

Budgeting: Implementing a realistic budget can help you manage your finances more effectively and ensure that you're living within your means. Set specific targets for reducing discretionary spending and increasing savings.

Skill Development: Invest in acquiring new skills or advancing your education to enhance your earning potential and career prospects. Consider short-term courses, workshops, or certifications that align with your interests and goals.

Savings Goals: Set targets for short-term savings goals, such as saving for a vacation, home improvement project, or major purchase.

Allocate a portion of your income toward these goals each month to make steady progress.

Long-Term Goals: Envisioning Your Financial Legacy

Long-term goals are the pinnacle of your financial vision, representing the culmination of years of strategic planning and disciplined execution. These goals typically have a timeline of five years or more and encompass your aspirations for financial independence, wealth accumulation, and legacy building. When setting long-term goals, consider the following:

Retirement Planning: Develop a comprehensive retirement plan that outlines your desired lifestyle in retirement, estimated expenses, and strategies for building a sufficient nest egg. Utilize retirement accounts such as 401(k)s, IRAs, or other investment vehicles to maximize tax advantages and investment growth.

Wealth Accumulation: Set ambitious targets for building wealth over the long term through strategic investing, real estate acquisition, entrepreneurship, or other wealth-building endeavours. Diversify your investment portfolio to mitigate risk and optimize returns.

Generational Wealth: Consider your legacy and how you can create lasting prosperity for future generations. Explore strategies such as estate planning, trusts, and charitable giving to preserve and transfer wealth to heirs or philanthropic causes.

Lifestyle Design: Envision your ideal lifestyle and set goals to achieve financial freedom and autonomy. This may include pursuing passions, traveling the world, or enjoying leisure activities without financial constraints.

Personal Growth: Invest in personal development and self-improvement to enhance your mindset, skills, and capabilities. Cultivate habits of lifelong learning, resilience, and adaptability to thrive in an ever-changing world.

As you identify both short-term and long-term goals, remember to make them SMART: Specific, Measurable, Achievable, Relevant, and Time-bound. Write down your goals, break them into actionable steps, and regularly review and revise them as needed.

In the next chapter, we'll explore the importance of setting specific, measurable, achievable, relevant, and time-bound (SMART) goals and how they serve as the roadmap for your journey to financial freedom. Until then, keep dreaming big, stay focused on your goals, and take consistent action toward realizing your financial aspirations.

Chapter 4

Setting Specific, Measurable, Achievable, Relevant, and Time-bound (SMART) Goals

Welcome to the cornerstone of your journey to financial freedom. In this chapter, we'll explore the transformative power of setting Specific, Measurable, Achievable, Relevant, and Time-bound (SMART) goals. The path to success is to take massive, determined action."

Specific: Clarity is Key

The first element of SMART goal setting is specificity. Your goals must be crystal clear and well-defined to provide you with a clear direction and purpose. Instead of vague aspirations like "I want to be rich," strive for specific goals such as "I want to achieve a net worth of $1 million within the next ten years."

When setting specific goals, consider the following:

What exactly do you want to achieve?
Why is this goal important to you?
What steps do you need to take to accomplish this goal?

By answering these questions, you'll gain clarity and focus, making it easier to devise a plan of action to achieve your objectives.

Measurable: Tracking Progress and Accountability

The second element of SMART goal setting is measurability. Your goals should be quantifiable, allowing you to track your progress and measure your success along the way. Instead of vague goals like "I want to save money," set measurable goals such as "I want to save $10,000 by the end of the year."

When setting measurable goals, consider the following:

How will you measure progress towards your goal?
What metrics will you use to determine success?
How frequently will you review your progress and adjust your strategy if necessary?

By establishing measurable criteria, you'll be able to hold yourself accountable and make informed decisions to stay on track towards achieving your goals.

Achievable: Balance Ambition with Realism

The third element of SMART goal setting is achievability. While it's essential to dream big and set ambitious goals, it's equally important to ensure that your goals are realistic and attainable given your current resources and circumstances. Instead of setting lofty goals like "I want to become a millionaire overnight," set achievable goals that stretch your limits but are within reach with effort and commitment.

When setting achievable goals, consider the following:

Are your goals aligned with your skills, capabilities, and resources?
What obstacles or challenges might you encounter along the way?
How will you overcome these obstacles and stay motivated in the face of adversity?

By striking the right balance between ambition and realism, you'll set yourself up for success and avoid the frustration of setting unattainable goals.

Relevant: Align Goals with Your Vision

The fourth element of SMART goal setting is relevance. Your goals should be relevant to your overarching vision of financial success and aligned with your values, priorities, and long-term aspirations. Instead of pursuing goals that don't resonate with your values or priorities, focus on goals that bring you closer to realizing your vision.

When setting relevant goals, consider the following:

How does this goal contribute to your overall vision of financial success?
Does this goal align with your values, priorities, and aspirations?
Will achieving this goal have a meaningful impact on your life and well-being?

By ensuring that your goals are relevant to your larger vision, you'll stay motivated and focused on what truly matters to you.

Time-Bound: Set Deadlines for Action

The fifth and final element of SMART goal setting is time-bound. Your goals should have clear deadlines or timeframes for completion, providing you with a sense of urgency and motivation to take action. Instead of open-ended goals like "Someday, I'll start saving for retirement," set specific deadlines such as "I'll max out my IRA contribution by the end of the year."

When setting time-bound goals, consider the following:

What is the deadline or timeframe for achieving this goal?

23

Is this deadline realistic given your resources and constraints?
How will you break down the goal into smaller milestones and set deadlines for each step?

By setting deadlines for action, you'll create a sense of urgency and momentum, driving you closer to your goals with purpose and determination.

In Summary: Your Roadmap to Success

Setting SMART goals is not just about wishful thinking; it's about taking deliberate and strategic action to turn your dreams into reality. By incorporating the principles of Specificity, Measurability, Achievability, Relevance, and Time-boundness into your goal-setting process, you'll create a roadmap to success that guides you toward financial freedom and abundance.

In the next chapter, we'll explore the process of prioritizing your financial objectives and developing a strategic plan to achieve your goals. Until then, take the time to reflect on your goals, refine them using the SMART criteria, and commit to taking decisive action towards realizing your vision of financial success. Your journey begins now, and the possibilities are endless.

Chapter 5
Prioritizing Your Financial Objectives

Welcome to the critical stage of your financial journey where we lay the groundwork for your future prosperity. In this chapter, we'll delve deep into the transformative process of prioritizing your financial objectives. The key to financial freedom and great wealth is a person's ability or skill to convert earned income into passive income and/or portfolio income.

Understanding the Importance of Prioritization

Prioritization is the art of determining the order of importance or urgency among a set of competing goals or tasks. In the context of financial planning, prioritizing your objectives is essential for allocating your resources - time, money, and energy - effectively and efficiently. By identifying and focusing on the most critical objectives first, you can make meaningful progress toward your long-term financial goals while avoiding distractions and unnecessary detours.

When it comes to prioritizing your financial objectives, consider the following key factors:

Impact: Evaluate the potential impact of each objective on your overall financial well-being. Focus on goals that will have the most significant positive effect on your financial situation, such as reducing debt, increasing savings, or building passive income streams.

Urgency: Assess the urgency of each objective and its timeline for completion. Prioritize goals that require immediate attention or have looming deadlines, such as paying off high-interest debt or establishing an emergency fund.

Alignment: Ensure that your objectives are aligned with your long-term vision of financial success and your core values. Focus on goals that resonate with your aspirations and priorities, rather than pursuing objectives that are incongruent with your goals or values.

Feasibility: Consider the feasibility and achievability of each objective given your current resources, capabilities, and constraints. Prioritize goals that are realistic and attainable within your means, while also challenging yourself to stretch beyond your comfort zone.

Identifying Your Top Financial Priorities

Now that you understand the principles of prioritization let's explore some common financial objectives and how to prioritize them effectively:

Debt Repayment: If you have high-interest debt, such as credit card balances or personal loans, prioritizing debt repayment should be your top financial priority. Allocate extra funds towards paying off these debts aggressively to free yourself from the burden of interest payments and move closer to financial freedom.

Emergency Fund: Building an emergency fund is crucial for protecting yourself against unexpected financial setbacks, such as job loss, medical emergencies, or car repairs. Prioritize saving for an emergency fund to ensure you have a financial safety net to fall back on during challenging times.

Retirement Savings: Planning for retirement should be a top priority, regardless of your age or career stage. Start by contributing to retirement accounts such as 401(k)s or IRAs and prioritize maximizing employer matching contributions to accelerate your savings growth.

Education and Skill Development: Investing in your education and skill development is essential for enhancing your earning potential and staying competitive in today's job market. Prioritize acquiring new skills or advancing your education to increase your income and career opportunities.

Wealth Accumulation: Building wealth through strategic investing, real estate acquisition, or entrepreneurship should be a long-term priority. Prioritize investing in assets that generate passive income or appreciation over time, such as stocks, bonds, real estate, or business ventures.

Developing a Strategic Plan of Action

Once you've identified your top financial priorities, it's time to develop a strategic plan of action to achieve them. Break down each objective into smaller, actionable steps and set specific deadlines for completion. Allocate your resources - time, money, and energy - according to the priority level of each objective, focusing on high-impact, high-urgency goals first.

Regularly review and reassess your financial priorities as your circumstances change and new opportunities or challenges arise. Stay flexible and adaptable, adjusting your plan as needed to stay on course towards your long-term financial goals.

In the next chapter, we'll explore the process of creating a comprehensive budget to support your financial objectives and maximize your resources.

Until then, take the time to reflect on your financial priorities and commit to taking decisive action to achieve them. Your financial future is in your hands, and the choices you make today will shape your destiny tomorrow.

Chapter 6
Breaking Down Goals into Actionable Steps

Welcome to the pivotal stage of your journey toward financial mastery, where we transform your aspirations into concrete actions. In this chapter, we'll delve deep into the transformative process of breaking down your goals into actionable steps. The key to success is to focus our conscious mind on things we desire, not things we fear.

Understanding the Power of Actionable Steps

Setting goals is just the beginning; the real magic happens when you translate those goals into specific, actionable steps. Actionable steps are the building blocks that bridge the gap between where you are now and where you want to be. By breaking down your goals into manageable tasks, you'll create a clear roadmap for success and empower yourself to take consistent action toward achieving your objectives.

When it comes to breaking down goals into actionable steps, consider the following key principles:

Clarity: Be crystal clear about what needs to be done to accomplish each goal. Define your action steps in precise terms, leaving no room for ambiguity or confusion.

Specificity: Break down your goals into small, specific tasks that are easy to understand and execute. Each action step should focus on a single aspect of your goal, making it easier to track progress and measure success.

Sequencing: Determine the logical sequence or order in which your action steps should be completed. Prioritize tasks based on their importance dependencies, and deadlines to ensure efficient progress toward your goal.

Realism: Be realistic about the time, resources, and effort required to complete each action step. Set yourself up for success by setting achievable milestones and avoiding overwhelm or burnout.

Accountability: Hold yourself accountable for completing each action step on time and to the best of your ability. Consider sharing your goals and progress with a trusted friend, family member, or mentor who can provide support and encouragement along the way.

Identifying Actionable Steps for Your Goals

Now that you understand the principles of breaking down goals into actionable steps, let's explore how to apply them to some common financial objectives:

Debt Repayment Goal: If your goal is to pay off $10,000 in credit card debt within one year, your actionable steps might include:

. Create a detailed list of all credit card balances and interest rates.
. Review your budget and identify areas where you can cut expenses to free up extra funds for debt repayment.
. Choose a debt repayment strategy, such as the debt snowball or debt avalanche method, and commit to making monthly payments above the minimum required.
. Set up automatic payments or reminders to ensure you never miss a payment deadline.

. Track your progress regularly and celebrate each milestone as you work towards becoming debt-free.

Emergency Fund Goal: If your goal is to save $5,000 for an emergency fund within six months, your actionable steps might include:

. Calculate how much you need to save each month to reach your target amount.
. Review your budget and identify areas where you can trim expenses or increase income to boost your savings rate.
. Open a high-yield savings account dedicated to your emergency fund and set up automatic transfers from your checking account.
. Monitor your savings progress regularly and adjust your plan as needed if unexpected expenses arise.
. Resist the temptation to dip into your emergency fund for non-essential purchases and prioritize building a financial safety net for future security.

Retirement Savings Goal: If your goal is to max out your annual 401(k) contribution of $19,500 within the calendar year, your actionable steps might include:

. Review your current 401(k) contribution rate and increase it to ensure you're on track to max out your annual limit.
. Calculate the amount you need to contribute each pay check to reach your target by the end of the year.
. Consider adjusting your budget to accommodate the increased contribution, reallocating funds from non-essential expenses to retirement savings.

. Monitor your progress regularly and adjust your contribution rate if necessary to stay on track towards reaching your goal.

. Take advantage of employer matching contributions to maximize the growth of your retirement nest egg.

Developing Your Action Plan

Now that you've identified actionable steps for your goals, it's time to develop a comprehensive action plan to guide your journey toward financial success. Organize your action steps into a logical sequence, setting deadlines and milestones for each task. Create a visual roadmap or checklist to track your progress and stay motivated as you work towards achieving your objectives.

In the next chapter, we'll explore the importance of creating a budget to support your financial goals and maximize your resources. Until then, take the time to break down your goals into actionable steps and commit to taking consistent action towards realizing your dreams. Remember, every small step you take brings you closer to the life of abundance and fulfilment you deserve.

Chapter 7

Creating a Budget
to Support Your Goals

Welcome to the cornerstone of financial success: budgeting. In this chapter, we'll delve deep into the transformative power of creating a budget to support your goals. It's not how much money you make, but how much money you keep, how hard it works for you, and how many generations you keep it for.

Understanding the Importance of Budgeting

Budgeting is not just about restricting your spending; it's about directing your financial resources towards what truly matters to you. It's the tool that helps you align your spending with your values, goals, and priorities. By creating a budget, you gain clarity and control over your finances, allowing you to make informed decisions that propel you towards your desired financial future.

Let's explore the key principles that underpin effective budgeting:

Awareness: The first step in creating a budget is gaining a clear understanding of your current financial situation. This involves tracking your income and expenses to identify patterns, trends, and areas where you can make improvements. Awareness is the foundation upon which you'll build your budgeting strategy.

Planning: Once you have a clear picture of your finances, it's time to develop a strategic plan for managing your money. This involves setting specific financial goals and creating a roadmap for how you will achieve them. Your budget serves as the blueprint for your financial success, guiding your spending and saving decisions.

Discipline: Budgeting requires discipline and self-control to stick to your financial plan even when faced with temptations or unexpected expenses. It's about making conscious choices about how you use your money and prioritizing your long-term financial well-being over short-term gratification.

Flexibility: While it's important to stick to your budget as much as possible, it's also essential to remain flexible and adaptable. Life is unpredictable, and your budget may need to be adjusted from time to time to accommodate changes in your circumstances or priorities. Stay open to making revisions as needed to ensure that your budget remains effective and relevant.

Creating Your Budget

Now that you understand the principles of budgeting, let's dive into the process of creating a budget that supports your financial goals:

Calculate Your Income: Start by calculating your total monthly income from all sources, including salaries, wages, bonuses, rental income, and any other sources of revenue. Be sure to account for your net income after taxes and deductions to get an accurate picture of your available funds.

Track Your Expenses: Next, track your monthly expenses in detail, categorizing them into essential and discretionary categories. Essential expenses include necessities such as housing, utilities, groceries, transportation, and healthcare, while discretionary expenses encompass non-essential purchases such as dining out, entertainment, and shopping.

Set Your Savings Goals: Determine how much you want to save each month towards your financial goals, such as building an emergency fund, paying off debt, or investing for retirement. Aim to save at least 10-20% of your income, if possible, and prioritize your savings goals based on their importance and urgency.

Allocate Your Resources: Once you've calculated your income and expenses, allocate your resources according to your priorities. Start by covering your essential expenses, then allocate funds towards your savings goals and debt repayment. Finally, allocate any remaining funds towards discretionary spending, being mindful of your long-term financial objectives.

Monitor and Adjust: Regularly monitor your budget and track your spending to ensure that you're staying on track towards your goals. Review your budget monthly and adjust your allocations as needed to accommodate changes in your income, expenses, or priorities.

Budgeting Tips for Success

To maximize the effectiveness of your budget and support your financial goals, consider the following tips:

Use Budgeting Tools: Take advantage of budgeting tools and apps to streamline the process of tracking your income and expenses. Many apps offer features such as automatic categorization, expense tracking, and goal setting to help you stay organized and on track.

Practice Frugality: Look for opportunities to reduce expenses and save money wherever possible. Cut back on non-essential purchases, negotiate lower bills, and seek out discounts and deals to stretch your dollars further.

Automate Your Finances: Set up automatic transfers and payments to ensure that you're consistently saving and paying bills on time. Automating your finances can help you stay disciplined and avoid the temptation to overspend.

Review Regularly: Schedule regular check-ins to review your budget and track your progress towards your goals. Use these reviews as an opportunity to identify areas for improvement and make adjustments as needed to stay on course.

By creating a budget that aligns with your financial goals and priorities, you'll take control of your finances and set yourself up for long-term success. In the next chapter, we'll explore strategies for reducing debt and freeing up financial resources to accelerate your journey towards financial freedom. Until then, take the time to create a budget that works for you and commit to managing your money wisely. Your future self will thank you for it.

Chapter 8
Establishing Emergency
Funds and Contingency Plans

Welcome to the critical stage of fortifying your financial fortress against unforeseen storms. In this chapter, we'll delve deep into the importance of establishing emergency funds and contingency plans. In today's rapidly changing world, the biggest risk is not taking any risk.

Understanding the Importance of Emergency Funds

Life is unpredictable, and unexpected expenses or emergencies can arise at any time. Whether it's a medical emergency, car repairs, or sudden job loss, having an emergency fund in place provides you with a financial safety net to weather the storm without derailing your long-term financial goals. Emergency funds provide peace of mind, stability, and resilience in the face of adversity, allowing you to navigate life's challenges with confidence and security.

Let's explore the key principles that underpin establishing emergency funds and contingency plans:

Preparedness: The first step in safeguarding your financial future is being prepared for the unexpected. Establishing an emergency fund ensures that you have cash reserves readily available to cover unexpected expenses or income disruptions without resorting to high-interest debt or depleting your savings.

Protection: Emergency funds protect you from financial setbacks and help prevent minor emergencies from spiralling into major crises. By having a financial buffer in place, you can handle unexpected expenses with ease and maintain your financial stability even during challenging times.

Peace of Mind: Knowing that you have a safety net in place provides peace of mind and reduces financial stress. Instead of worrying about how you'll cover unexpected expenses, you can focus on your long-term financial goals and pursue opportunities for growth and prosperity.

Opportunity: Having an emergency fund gives you the freedom and flexibility to seize opportunities when they arise. Whether it's investing in a promising opportunity, pursuing further education, or starting a new business venture, having cash reserves allows you to take calculated risks and pursue your dreams with confidence.

Establishing Your Emergency Fund

Now that you understand the importance of emergency funds let's explore how to establish one that meets your needs:

Determine Your Target Amount: Start by determining how much you need to save for your emergency fund. Aim to save at least three to six months' worth of living expenses to cover essential costs such as housing, utilities, groceries, transportation, and healthcare.

Set a Savings Goal: Break down your target amount into manageable savings goals and set a timeline for achieving them. Determine how much you need to save each month to reach your target within a reasonable timeframe and commit to making regular contributions to your emergency fund.

Automate Your Savings: Set up automatic transfers from your checking account to your emergency fund to ensure consistent and disciplined saving.

Treat your emergency fund contributions as non-negotiable expenses and prioritize them just like you would your other financial obligations.

Keep Your Funds Accessible: Store your emergency fund in a highly liquid and easily accessible account, such as a high-yield savings account or money market fund. While it's essential to earn a competitive interest rate on your savings, prioritize accessibility and liquidity over higher returns.

Creating Contingency Plans

In addition to establishing emergency funds, it's essential to create contingency plans for potential emergencies or disruptions:

Health Emergencies: Review your health insurance coverage and consider purchasing additional coverage or supplemental insurance to protect yourself and your family from unexpected medical expenses. Research healthcare options and providers in your area to ensure prompt access to quality care when needed.

Job Loss: Develop a plan for managing a sudden loss of income, such as unemployment benefits, severance packages, or alternative income sources. Consider updating your resume, networking with industry contacts, and exploring freelance or part-time opportunities to supplement your income during a job transition.

Natural Disasters: Prepare for natural disasters or other emergencies by creating a disaster preparedness kit, establishing evacuation plans, and securing important documents and valuables. Stay informed about local emergency protocols and evacuation procedures and have a communication plan in place for staying in touch with family members during emergencies.

Financial Hardships: Anticipate potential financial hardships, such as economic downturns or market fluctuations, by diversifying your income sources and investment portfolio. Maintain a conservative approach to debt and spending and build resilience by living below your means and maintaining a healthy savings cushion.

By establishing emergency funds and contingency plans, you'll fortify your financial resilience and protect yourself from unforeseen emergencies or disruptions. In the next chapter, we'll explore strategies for reducing debt and freeing up financial resources to accelerate your journey towards financial freedom. Until then, take the time to establish your emergency fund and contingency plans and commit to safeguarding your financial future. Your peace of mind and financial security depend on it.

Chapter 9
Aligning Your Goals with Your Values and Lifestyle

Welcome to the heart of your financial journey, where we explore the profound connection between your goals, values, and lifestyle. In this chapter, we'll delve deep into the transformative process of aligning your financial objectives with what truly matters to you. Success is not just about making money; it's about making a difference and living a life of purpose.

Understanding the Importance of Alignment

Aligning your goals with your values and lifestyle is the secret sauce to achieving true wealth and fulfilment. It's about more than just accumulating wealth; it's about creating a life that reflects your core values, passions, and aspirations. When your financial goals are aligned with what matters most to you, you'll experience a profound sense of purpose and satisfaction, driving you towards success with clarity and conviction.

Let's explore the key principles that underpin aligning your goals with your values and lifestyle:

Self-Reflection: The first step in aligning your goals with your values is self-reflection. Take the time to identify your core values, beliefs, and priorities. What matters most to you in life? What brings you joy, fulfilment, and meaning? Understanding your values will guide you in setting goals that are meaningful and authentic to you.

Visioning: Envision the life you want to create for yourself and your loved ones. What does success look like to you? What are your dreams and aspirations? Visualize your ideal lifestyle and use this vision as a compass to guide your financial decisions and actions.

Purpose: Connect your financial goals to a higher purpose or mission that aligns with your values. How do your goals contribute to your personal growth, family well-being, or community impact? When your goals are rooted in purpose, you'll feel a deep sense of motivation and commitment to achieving them.

Flexibility: Be open to adapting your goals and plans as your values and priorities evolve over time. Life is dynamic, and what may be important to you today may change tomorrow. Stay flexible and responsive to new opportunities, challenges, and insights that arise along your journey.

Aligning Your Goals with Your Values and Lifestyle

Now that you understand the principles of alignment let's explore how to apply them to your financial goals:

Identify Your Values: Start by identifying your core values and beliefs. What principles guide your decisions and actions? Common values include family, health, freedom, creativity, integrity, and contribution. Take the time to clarify your values and prioritize them in order of importance.

Define Your Goals: Once you've identified your values, use them as a foundation for setting your financial goals. Ask yourself: How can I align my goals with my values? For example, if family is a core value, your goals may include saving for your children's education, purchasing a home where you can create lasting memories, or providing financial support for aging parents.

Assess Your Lifestyle: Take a close look at your current lifestyle and spending habits. Are your expenses aligned with your values and goals, or are you spending money on things that don't bring you true satisfaction or fulfilment? Identify areas where you can reallocate resources to support your highest priorities.

Make Conscious Choices: As you set goals and make financial decisions, be intentional about aligning them with your values and lifestyle. Ask yourself: Does this expense or investment support my values and goals? Will it bring me closer to the life I envision for myself? By making conscious choices, you'll ensure that your actions are in harmony with your deepest desires.

Continuously Evaluate and Adjust: Regularly review your goals, values, and lifestyle to ensure alignment and make adjustments as needed. As you grow and evolve, your priorities may shift, requiring you to realign your goals accordingly. Stay attuned to your inner wisdom and intuition, and trust that you have the power to create the life you desire.

In Summary

Aligning your goals with your values and lifestyle is the key to unlocking true wealth and fulfilment. By infusing your financial journey with purpose, meaning, and authenticity, you'll experience a profound sense of satisfaction and joy as you work towards achieving your dreams. Remember, wealth is not just about what you have; it's about who you are and how you live your life. In the next chapter, we'll explore strategies for leveraging your assets and investments to create passive income stream s that support your desired lifestyle. Until then, take the time to reflect on your values and align your goals accordingly. Your future self will thank you for it.

Chapter 10

Overcoming Common Obstacles to Goal Setting

Welcome to the battlefield of your financial journey, where we confront the obstacles that stand between you and your goals. In this chapter, we'll explore the common challenges that many face when setting and pursuing financial goals, and we'll arm you with the strategies you need to overcome them. The size of your success is measured by the strength of your desire, the size of your dream, and how you handle disappointment along the way.

Understanding the Importance of Goal Setting

Goal setting is the compass that guides you towards your desired destination. It's the process of defining your objectives, breaking them down into manageable steps, and taking consistent action to achieve them. However, despite its importance, many individuals encounter obstacles that hinder their ability to set and pursue their financial goals effectively.

Let's explore some common obstacles to goal setting and how to overcome them:

Fear of Failure: One of the most significant obstacles to goal setting is the fear of failure. Many individuals hesitate to set ambitious goals for fear of falling short or facing disappointment. However, failure is not the opposite of success; it's a stepping stone on the path to success. Embrace failure as a learning opportunity and a necessary part of the journey towards your goals.

Lack of Clarity: Another common obstacle is a lack of clarity about what you want to achieve and why it's important to you. Without clear objectives, it's challenging to stay motivated and focused on taking action towards your goals. Take the time to define your goals with precision and articulate why they matter to you.

Visualize your desired outcomes and keep them at the forefront of your mind as you work towards them.

Procrastination: Procrastination is the enemy of progress when it comes to goal setting. Many individuals delay taking action towards their goals, waiting for the "perfect" time or conditions to begin. However, there is no perfect time to start pursuing your goals; the time is now. Break your goals down into small, manageable steps, and take action every day, even if it's just a small step forward.

Lack of Accountability: Without accountability, it's easy to lose motivation and veer off course from your goals. Many individuals struggle to hold themselves accountable for their actions and fail to follow through on their commitments. Find an accountability partner or join a mastermind group to keep you motivated and on track towards your goals. Share your goals with others and ask for support and encouragement along the way.

External Obstacles: In addition to internal obstacles, such as fear and procrastination, you may also encounter external obstacles that hinder your progress towards your goals. These obstacles could include financial constraints, time limitations, or unexpected life events. While you may not be able to control these external factors, you can control how you respond to them. Stay flexible and adaptable and be willing to adjust your approach as needed to overcome obstacles and stay on course towards your goals.

Strategies for Overcoming Obstacles

Now that we've identified some common obstacles to goal setting let's explore some strategies for overcoming them:

Break Down Your Goals: Break your goals down into smaller, more manageable tasks that you can tackle one step at a time. Focus on making progress every day, no matter how small, and celebrate each milestone along the way.

Cultivate a Growth Mindset: Embrace a growth mindset and see challenges as opportunities for growth and learning. Instead of viewing setbacks as failures, see them as valuable feedback that can help you improve and progress towards your goals.

Visualize Success: Visualize yourself achieving your goals with clarity and detail. Create a vision board or visualization exercise that allows you to see and feel what it will be like to accomplish your goals. Use this visualization to stay motivated and focused on your objectives.

Find Support: Surround yourself with a supportive network of friends, family, mentors, and peers who believe in your potential and encourage you to pursue your goals. Lean on this support network for guidance, advice, and encouragement when you encounter obstacles along the way.

Take Action: The most important step in overcoming obstacles is to take action. Instead of allowing fear, doubt, or uncertainty to hold you back, take decisive action towards your goals. Remember, the journey of a thousand miles begins with a single step.

In Summary

Overcoming obstacles to goal setting is a critical aspect of achieving financial success.

Overcoming Common
Obstacles to Goal Setting

By recognizing and addressing common challenges such as fear of failure, lack of clarity, procrastination, lack of accountability, and external obstacles, you can unlock your full potential and move closer towards your goals. Stay focused, stay resilient, and remember that every obstacle you overcome brings you one step closer to the life of abundance and fulfilment you desire. In the next chapter, we'll explore strategies for staying motivated and maintaining momentum on your journey towards financial success. Until then, keep pushing forward, and never lose sight of your goals.

Chapter 11
Staying Motivated and Persistent Throughout the Process

Welcome to the inner sanctum of your financial journey, where we uncover the secrets to staying motivated and persistent in the pursuit of your goals. In this chapter, we'll explore the mindset and strategies necessary to overcome obstacles, navigate setbacks, and maintain unwavering determination on your path to financial success. The size of your success is measured by the strength of your desire, the size of your dream, and how you handle disappointment along the way.

Understanding the Importance of Motivation and Persistence

Motivation and persistence are the twin engines that drive you towards your goals, even in the face of adversity. They fuel your determination, resilience, and perseverance, enabling you to overcome obstacles and stay focused on your desired outcomes. Without motivation and persistence, even the most well-defined goals and strategies are doomed to falter.

Let's explore the key principles that underpin staying motivated and persistent throughout the process:

Clarity of Purpose: The first step in staying motivated and persistent is having a clear sense of purpose and direction. Understand why your goals matter to you and how achieving them aligns with your values, aspirations, and vision for the future. When your goals are deeply meaningful and connected to your purpose, you'll find the inner drive to keep pushing forward, no matter what challenges arise.

Resilience in the Face of Setbacks: Setbacks and obstacles are inevitable on the path to success, but it's how you respond to them that determines your outcome.

Cultivate resilience by reframing setbacks as learning opportunities and maintaining a positive outlook in the face of adversity. See challenges as stepping stones on your journey rather than roadblocks and keep moving forward with determination and optimism.

Discipline and Consistency: Discipline and consistency are the cornerstones of success in any endeavour. Stay committed to your goals by establishing daily habits and routines that support your progress. Break your goals down into smaller, manageable tasks, and commit to taking consistent action towards them every day. Even on days when you don't feel motivated, show up and do the work—your future self will thank you for it.

Celebrate Milestones and Progress: Celebrate your achievements and milestones along the way to keep your motivation high. Acknowledge and reward yourself for your hard work, perseverance, and progress towards your goals. Celebrating small wins not only boosts your morale but also reinforces positive habits and behaviours that contribute to your success.

Surround Yourself with Support: Surround yourself with a supportive network of friends, family, mentors, and peers who believe in your potential and encourage you to pursue your goals. Lean on this support network for guidance, advice, and encouragement when you encounter challenges or setbacks. Having a strong support system can provide you with the motivation and inspiration you need to keep going when the going gets tough.

Strategies for Staying Motivated and Persistent

Now that we've explored the principles of motivation and persistence let's explore some strategies for cultivating and sustaining them:

Set Inspiring Goals: Set goals that inspire and excite you, and that align with your values, passions, and aspirations. When your goals are deeply meaningful and connected to your purpose, you'll find the inner drive to stay motivated and persistent, even when faced with challenges.

Visualize Success: Visualize yourself achieving your goals with clarity and detail. Create a vision board or visualization exercise that allows you to see and feel what it will be like to accomplish your goals. Use this visualization to stay motivated and focused on your objectives, even during times of doubt or uncertainty.

Break Down Your Goals: Break your goals down into smaller, more manageable tasks that you can tackle one step at a time. Focus on making progress every day, no matter how small, and celebrate each milestone along the way. By breaking your goals down into bite-sized pieces, you'll avoid feeling overwhelmed and stay motivated to keep moving forward.

Stay Flexible and Adapt: Stay flexible and adaptable in your approach to achieving your goals. Be willing to adjust your strategies, timelines, and expectations as needed to overcome obstacles and navigate changes in your circumstances. Remember, it's not about how quickly you reach your goals but how persistently you pursue them.

Cultivate Self-Compassion: Be kind and compassionate towards yourself, especially during times of struggle or setback. Recognize that setbacks are a natural part of the journey towards success, and that you are doing the best you can with the resources and knowledge you have. Treat yourself with the same patience, understanding, and encouragement that you would offer to a friend facing similar challenges.

In Summary

Staying motivated and persistent throughout the process is essential for achieving your financial goals and realizing your dreams. By cultivating a clear sense of purpose, resilience in the face of setbacks, discipline and consistency in your actions, and a supportive network of allies, you'll fuel your journey towards success with unwavering determination and resolve. Remember, success is not a destination but a journey - a journey fuelled by passion, perseverance, and the relentless pursuit of your dreams. In the next chapter, we'll explore the power of continuous learning and growth in accelerating your journey towards financial mastery. Until then, keep the fire of motivation burning bright within you, and never lose sight of the incredible potential that lies within your reach.

Chapter 12
Celebrating Milestones and Progress Along the Way

Welcome to the stage of your financial journey where we honour the milestones and victories that pave the path to success. In this chapter, we'll explore the transformative power of celebrating progress and how it fuels your motivation to reach greater heights. Celebrate your successes. Find some humour in your failures. Take some deep breaths. And realize that you can, indeed, accomplish anything.

Understanding the Importance of Celebration

Celebrating milestones and progress along the way is not just about throwing a party or patting yourself on the back—it's about acknowledging your achievements and recognizing the hard work, dedication, and perseverance that went into reaching them. Celebration serves as fuel for your motivation, boosting your confidence, morale, and resilience, and propelling you forward towards even greater success.

Let's delve deeper into why celebrating milestones and progress is so crucial:

Acknowledgment: The first step in celebrating milestones and progress is acknowledging your achievements, no matter how small. Take the time to reflect on your progress and recognize the milestones you've reached, whether it's paying off a debt, reaching a savings goal, or making your first investment. Acknowledgment is the foundation upon which celebration is built.

Motivation: Celebration serves as a powerful motivator, inspiring you to continue pushing forward towards your goals. When you celebrate your achievements, you reinforce positive behaviours and habits, and strengthen your belief in your ability to succeed.

Celebrating progress fuels your motivation, keeping you focused, energized, and determined to reach even greater heights.

Gratitude: Celebration cultivates an attitude of gratitude, helping you appreciate the journey as much as the destination. When you take the time to celebrate your victories, you express gratitude for the blessings, opportunities, and support that have contributed to your success. Gratitude breeds abundance and attracts more blessings into your life, creating a positive cycle of growth and prosperity.

Reflection: Celebration provides an opportunity for reflection, allowing you to pause and savour the moment before moving forward. Take the time to reflect on the lessons you've learned, the obstacles you've overcome, and the growth you've experienced along the way. Reflection deepens your understanding of yourself and your journey and prepares you for the challenges and opportunities that lie ahead.

Celebrating Milestones and Progress

Now that we understand the importance of celebration let's explore how to celebrate milestones and progress along the way:

Set Milestones: Break your long-term goals down into smaller, more manageable milestones that you can celebrate along the way. For example, if your goal is to save $10,000 for a down payment on a house, set milestones at $2,500, $5,000, and $7,500, and celebrate each milestone as you reach it.

Choose Meaningful Rewards: Celebrate your milestones with rewards that are meaningful and aligned with your values and priorities.

This could be anything from treating yourself to a special dinner, taking a day off to relax and recharge, or investing in something that brings you joy and fulfilment.

Share Your Success: Share your achievements with friends, family, and mentors who have supported you along the way. Celebrating your milestones with others not only allows you to express gratitude for their support but also inspires and motivates them to pursue their own goals with renewed Vigor.

Reflect and Renew: Take the time to reflect on your progress and the lessons you've learned along the way. Use this reflection as fuel for your continued growth and development, and as inspiration to set new goals and pursue even greater challenges.

Celebrating milestones and progress along the way is not just a reward for your hard work - it's an essential component of your journey towards financial mastery. By acknowledging your achievements, fuelling your motivation, and fostering an attitude of gratitude, you'll propel yourself forward towards greater success with confidence and determination.

In the next chapter, we'll explore the power of continuous learning and growth in accelerating your journey towards financial mastery. We'll delve into strategies for expanding your knowledge, developing new skills, and staying ahead of the curve in an ever-changing world. Until then, take the time to celebrate your milestones and progress, and remember to savour the journey as much as the destination. Your future self will thank you for it.

Chapter 13
Reviewing and Adjusting Goals as Needed

Welcome to the helm of your financial voyage, where we chart the course through the dynamic waters of goal setting. In this chapter, we'll explore the vital practice of reviewing and adjusting your goals to ensure they remain aligned with your aspirations and the changing currents of life. The only constant in life is change, and the most successful individuals are those who embrace it and adapt accordingly.

Understanding the Importance of Review and Adjustment

Setting goals is not a one-time event but an ongoing process that requires regular review and adjustment. The journey towards financial success is marked by twists, turns, and unexpected detours, and your goals must evolve to reflect these changes. Reviewing and adjusting your goals allows you to stay flexible, responsive, and aligned with your ever-evolving vision and circumstances.

Let's delve deeper into why reviewing and adjusting goals is so crucial:

Adaptation: Life is full of surprises, both pleasant and challenging, and your goals must adapt to accommodate these changes. By regularly reviewing and adjusting your goals, you ensure they remain relevant and achievable in light of shifting priorities, opportunities, and constraints.

Optimization: Reviewing and adjusting your goals allows you to optimize your efforts and resources for maximum impact. You may discover new insights, strategies, or resources that enable you to achieve your goals more efficiently or effectively. By staying proactive and responsive, you can continually fine-tune your goals to maximize your chances of success.

Alignment: As you grow and evolve personally and professionally, your values, priorities, and aspirations may shift. Reviewing and adjusting your goals ensures they remain aligned with your current values and aspirations, allowing you to pursue objectives that are truly meaningful and fulfilling to you.

Course Correction: Even the best-laid plans can go awry, and it's essential to course-correct when necessary. By regularly reviewing your progress towards your goals, you can identify potential obstacles or setbacks early on and take proactive measures to address them. Adjusting your goals allows you to stay on track and navigate around obstacles with confidence and resilience.

Reviewing and Adjusting Goals as Needed

Now that we understand the importance of review and adjustment, let's explore how to incorporate this practice into your financial journey:

Establish a Review Schedule: Set aside regular intervals - such as quarterly, semi-annually, or annually - to review your progress towards your goals. Use these review sessions as an opportunity to reflect on your achievements, reassess your priorities, and adjust your goals as needed.

Evaluate Your Progress: During your review sessions, evaluate your progress towards each of your goals. Are you on track to achieve them within your desired timeframe? Have any unforeseen challenges arisen that require you to adjust your approach? Be honest with yourself about your progress and identify areas where you may need to course-correct.

Reassess Your Priorities: Life is dynamic, and your priorities may shift over time.

Take the time to reassess your values, aspirations, and long-term objectives, and ensure your goals are aligned with your current priorities. Are there any goals that are no longer meaningful or relevant to you? Are there new goals or aspirations you'd like to pursue?

Make Adjustments: Based on your review and reassessment, make any necessary adjustments to your goals. This could involve revising timelines, reallocating resources, or setting new objectives altogether. Be flexible and open-minded in your approach and prioritize goals that are most important and meaningful to you.

Reviewing and adjusting your goals as needed is a critical aspect of your journey towards financial mastery. By staying proactive, flexible, and aligned with your values and aspirations, you'll ensure that your goals remain relevant, achievable, and fulfilling over time.

In the next chapter, we'll explore the value of seeking professional advice and guidance to help you navigate the complexities of the financial landscape. We'll delve into the benefits of working with experts, such as financial advisors, accountants, and lawyers, and how their insights and expertise can empower you to make informed decisions and achieve your goals with confidence. Until then, take the time to review and adjust your goals as needed, and remember that adaptability is the key to success in an ever-changing world.

Chapter 14

Seeking Professional
Advice and Guidance

Welcome to the helm of your ship, where we explore the importance of seeking professional advice and guidance to navigate the sometimes-treacherous waters of the financial world. In this chapter, we'll uncover the invaluable insights and expertise that professionals can provide, helping you chart a course towards financial success with confidence and clarity. richest people in the world look for and build networks; everyone else looks for work.

Understanding the Importance of Professional Advice

In the vast and complex landscape of finance, seeking professional advice and guidance is akin to enlisting the services of skilled navigators to guide you through uncharted waters. Whether you're navigating investments, taxes, estate planning, or other financial matters, professionals bring specialized knowledge, experience, and perspective to help you make informed decisions and avoid potential pitfalls.

Let's delve deeper into why seeking professional advice and guidance is so crucial:

Expertise: Financial professionals, such as financial advisors, accountants, lawyers, and estate planners, possess specialized knowledge and expertise in their respective fields. They can provide insights and strategies tailored to your unique circumstances and goals, helping you navigate complex financial matters with confidence and competence.

Objectivity: Emotions often cloud judgment when it comes to money matters, leading to irrational decisions and missed opportunities. Financial professionals offer an objective perspective, free from emotional biases, to help you make rational, data-driven decisions that align with your long-term goals and priorities.

Strategy: Building wealth and achieving financial security require strategic planning and execution. Financial professionals can help you develop comprehensive financial plans, investment strategies, and tax optimization strategies tailored to your goals, risk tolerance, and time horizon. By aligning your actions with a strategic roadmap, you can maximize your chances of success and minimize unnecessary risks.

Compliance: The financial landscape is rife with regulations, tax laws, and compliance requirements that can be daunting to navigate on your own. Financial professionals can help you stay compliant with relevant laws and regulations, ensuring that you avoid costly penalties and legal pitfalls.

Seeking Professional Advice and Guidance

Now that we understand the importance of professional advice let's explore how to leverage the expertise of financial professionals:

Assess Your Needs: Start by assessing your financial situation, goals, and areas where you could benefit from professional guidance. Do you need help with investment planning, retirement planning, tax optimization, estate planning, or all of the above? Identifying your needs will help you determine which type of professional to seek out.

Choose Wisely: When selecting financial professionals, take the time to research and interview potential candidates to ensure they have the expertise, credentials, and track record of success in addressing your specific needs.

Look for professionals who are fiduciaries, meaning they are legally obligated to act in your best interests.

Build a Team: Financial planning is a collaborative effort that often requires input from multiple professionals, each with their own area of expertise. Consider building a team of professionals, such as a financial advisor, accountant, lawyer, and estate planner, to provide comprehensive guidance and support across all aspects of your financial life.

Communicate Effectively: Establish open and transparent communication with your financial professionals, and clearly articulate your goals, concerns, and expectations. Be proactive in seeking their advice and guidance, and don't hesitate to ask questions or voice any uncertainties you may have. Effective communication is essential for building trust and ensuring that your financial professionals understand your needs and objectives.

Seeking professional advice and guidance is a vital component of your journey towards financial mastery. By leveraging the expertise of financial professionals, you can gain valuable insights, develop strategic plans, and navigate complex financial matters with confidence and clarity.

In the next chapter, we'll explore the power of leveraging technology and tools to track your progress towards your goals. We'll delve into the benefits of using digital platforms, apps, and software to monitor your finances, track your investments and stay organized and informed in real-time. Until then, consider reaching out to financial professionals to help you chart a course towards financial success, and remember that expert guidance can make all the difference in achieving your goals.

Chapter 15
Leveraging Technology and Tools to Track Your Progress

In this chapter, we'll explore how to harness the power of technology and tools to track your progress towards financial success with precision and efficiency. It's not the smart that get ahead, but the bold.

Understanding the Importance of Technology and Tools

In today's digital age, technology has revolutionized the way we manage our finances, offering a plethora of tools and platforms to streamline processes, automate tasks, and gain valuable insights into our financial health. By leveraging technology effectively, you can track your progress towards your goals in real-time, identify areas for improvement, and make data-driven decisions to optimize your financial journey.

Let's delve deeper into why leveraging technology and tools is so crucial:

Real-Time Visibility: Technology provides real-time visibility into your financial situation, allowing you to track your income, expenses, investments, and net worth at a glance. With digital tools, you can access up-to-date financial information anytime, anywhere, empowering you to make informed decisions on the fly.

Organization and Efficiency: Digital tools help streamline financial tasks, automate routine processes, and reduce manual paperwork, saving you time and effort. From budgeting apps to investment tracking platforms, technology allows you to organize your finances efficiently and stay on top of your financial obligations with ease.

Goal Tracking: Many digital platforms offer goal tracking features that allow you to set, monitor, and track progress towards your financial goals. Whether you're saving for a down payment, paying off debt, or building an emergency fund, technology provides the tools you need to stay focused and motivated on achieving your objectives.

Data Analysis: Technology enables advanced data analysis and reporting capabilities, allowing you to gain valuable insights into your financial performance and behaviour. With data-driven analytics, you can identify trends, patterns, and areas for improvement in your financial habits, and make adjustments to optimize your outcomes.

Leveraging Technology and Tools

Now that we understand the importance of technology let's explore how to leverage digital tools to track your progress towards financial success:

Choose the Right Tools: Start by selecting digital tools and platforms that align with your specific needs, goals, and preferences. Whether you're looking for budgeting apps, investment trackers, expense management software, or all of the above, research and compare different options to find the best fit for you.

Automate Routine Tasks: Take advantage of automation features offered by digital tools to streamline routine financial tasks, such as bill payments, expense categorization, and savings transfers. By automating repetitive processes, you can free up time and mental energy to focus on more strategic aspects of your financial management.

Set Up Alerts and Reminders: Use alerts and reminders provided by digital tools to stay on top of important deadlines, payments, and financial milestones.

Set Up Alerts and Reminders: Use alerts and reminders provided by digital tools to stay on top of important deadlines, payments, and financial milestones. Whether it's a notification for an upcoming bill payment, a reminder to review your investment portfolio, or an alert for reaching a savings goal, technology can help keep you accountable and on track towards your goals.

Monitor Your Progress: Regularly review and monitor your financial progress using the tracking and reporting features offered by digital tools. Track your income, expenses, savings, investments, and net worth over time to gauge your performance and identify areas for improvement. Use this data to make informed decisions and adjust your strategies as needed to stay on course towards your goals.

Leveraging technology and tools to track your progress is a powerful strategy for optimizing your financial journey. By harnessing the power of digital navigation, you can gain real-time visibility into your finances, streamline processes, and make data-driven decisions to achieve your goals with confidence and efficiency.

In the next chapter, we'll explore the importance of surrounding yourself with a supportive network of friends, family, mentors, and peers who believe in your potential and encourage you to pursue your goals. We'll delve into the benefits of building a strong support system and how it can empower you to overcome obstacles, stay motivated, and achieve greater success in your financial endeavours. Until then, embrace the power of technology to navigate your financial journey and remember that the digital tools at your disposal are the wind in your sails as you chart a course towards financial mastery.

Chapter 16
Surrounding Yourself with a Supportive Network

Welcome to the harbour of camaraderie, where we explore the importance of surrounding yourself with a supportive network of allies to navigate the complexities of the financial world. In this chapter, we'll delve into the transformative power of building a strong support system and how it can propel you towards greater success on your financial journey. The richest people in the world look for and build networks; everyone else looks for work.

Understanding the Importance of a Supportive Network

In the unpredictable and often challenging journey towards financial success, having a supportive network of friends, family, mentors, and peers can make all the difference. Allies provide encouragement, guidance, accountability, and perspective, helping you overcome obstacles, stay motivated, and achieve your goals with confidence and resilience.

Let's delve deeper into why surrounding yourself with a supportive network is so crucial:

Encouragement and Motivation: A supportive network provides encouragement and motivation during both the highs and lows of your financial journey. Allies cheer you on during successes, offer words of encouragement during setbacks, and remind you of your strengths and potential when doubt creeps in. Their unwavering support fuels your determination and resilience, helping you stay focused on your goals even in the face of adversity.

Guidance and Mentorship: Mentors and experienced individuals within your network offers invaluable guidance and mentorship, sharing their wisdom, insights, and lessons learned from their own financial journeys. They provide perspective, challenge your assumptions, and offer practical advice to help you navigate complex financial decisions and avoid common pitfalls. By learning from their experiences, you can accelerate your own growth and avoid repeating mistakes.

Accountability and Challenge: Allies hold you accountable to your goals, challenging you to stretch beyond your comfort zone and reach for greater heights. They provide honest feedback, hold up a mirror to your actions and behaviours, and challenge you to confront your fears and limiting beliefs. Their constructive criticism pushes you to grow, adapt, and strive for excellence in pursuit of your goals.

Emotional Support: Financial management can be stressful and overwhelming at times, and allies provide essential emotional support to help you navigate the ups and downs of the journey. They offer a listening ear, a shoulder to lean on, and a source of comfort and reassurance during moments of doubt, uncertainty, or anxiety. Knowing that you're not alone in your struggles strengthens your resolve and resilience, enabling you to persevere through challenges with grace and determination.

Surrounding Yourself with a Supportive Network

Now that we understand the importance of a supportive network let's explore how to cultivate and leverage allies on your financial journey:

Identify Your Allies: Start by identifying individuals within your existing network who share your values, aspirations, and commitment to financial success.

Look for friends, family members, colleagues, mentors, and peers who have a positive mindset, a growth-oriented outlook, and a willingness to support and encourage your goals.

Cultivate Relationships: Invest time and effort into cultivating meaningful relationships with your allies, building trust, rapport, and mutual respect. Be genuine, empathetic, and supportive in your interactions, and demonstrate your willingness to listen, learn, and reciprocate their support. By nurturing strong connections with your allies, you create a supportive ecosystem that fosters growth, collaboration, and mutual success.

Seek Out Mentors: Actively seek out mentors and experienced individuals within your network who can offer guidance, wisdom, and perspective on your financial journey. Approach potential mentors with humility, respect, and a genuine desire to learn from their experiences. Be open to feedback, advice, and constructive criticism, and demonstrate your commitment to applying their insights to your own growth and development.

Be a Supportive Ally: In addition to receiving support from your allies, be a supportive ally in return. Offer encouragement, guidance, and assistance to others who are on their own financial journeys and celebrate their successes as enthusiastically as you celebrate your own. By being a source of support and inspiration to others, you strengthen your bonds within the network and contribute to a culture of mutual empowerment and growth.

Surrounding yourself with a supportive network is a cornerstone of success on your financial journey. By cultivating strong relationships with allies who provide encouragement, guidance, accountability, and emotional support, you create a powerful ecosystem that propels you towards your goals with confidence and resilience.

In the next chapter, we'll explore the importance of incorporating financial education and skill-building into your plan for financial success. We'll delve into strategies for expanding your knowledge, developing new skills, and staying ahead of the curve in an ever-changing financial landscape. Until then, continue to nurture and leverage your supportive network, and remember that together, we rise higher than we ever could alone.

Chapter 17
Incorporating Financial Education Skill Building into Your Plan

In this chapter, we'll delve into the importance of incorporating financial education and skill building into your plan, equipping you with the knowledge and expertise needed to navigate the complex terrain of the financial world. The more you learn, the more you earn.

Understanding the Importance of Financial Education

In today's fast-paced and ever-changing world, financial literacy is more crucial than ever before. Yet, many individuals lack the knowledge and skills necessary to make informed financial decisions, leading to missed opportunities, financial setbacks, and even crisis. Incorporating financial education and skill building into your plan is essential for empowering yourself to take control of your financial future and achieve lasting success.

Let's delve deeper into why financial education is so crucial:

Empowerment: Financial education empowers you with the knowledge and skills needed to make informed decisions about money matters. By understanding fundamental concepts such as budgeting, investing, debt management, and retirement planning, you gain greater control over your financial destiny and can confidently navigate the complexities of the financial world.

Risk Mitigation: Financial education helps you identify and mitigate potential risks and pitfalls in your financial journey. Whether it's recognizing predatory financial products, avoiding investment scams, or understanding the implications of debt, a solid foundation of financial knowledge enables you to protect yourself and your assets from unnecessary risks and losses.

Opportunity Recognition: Financial education opens your eyes to the multitude of opportunities available for building wealth and achieving financial success. By learning about different investment vehicles, asset classes, and financial strategies, you can identify opportunities for growth and take advantage of them to enhance your financial position and secure your future.

Lifelong Learning: The financial landscape is constantly evolving, with new technologies, regulations, and market trends shaping the way we manage our money. Financial education is not a one-time event but a lifelong journey of learning and growth. By committing to ongoing education and skill building, you can stay informed, adaptable, and ahead of the curve in an ever-changing world.

Incorporating Financial Education and Skill Building into Your Plan

Now that we understand the importance of financial education let's explore how to incorporate it into your plan for financial success:

Set Learning Goals: Start by setting specific learning goals related to financial education and skill building. Identify areas where you need to improve your knowledge and expertise, such as budgeting, investing, tax planning, or estate planning, and set goals for acquiring the necessary skills and information.

Invest in Education: Take advantage of a wide range of educational resources and opportunities available to you, including books, podcasts, online courses, workshops, seminars, and certifications.

Invest time and resources into expanding your financial knowledge and skill set and prioritize continuous learning as a key component of your financial plan.

Seek Mentorship: Surround yourself with mentors, advisors, and experts who can provide guidance, support, and wisdom based on their own experiences and expertise. Seek out mentors who have achieved the level of financial success you aspire to, and learn from their insights, lessons, and advice.

Practice Hands-On Learning: Apply what you learn through hands-on practice and real-world experience. Experiment with budgeting tools, investment platforms, and financial planning software to gain practical skills and confidence in managing your finances. Don't be afraid to make mistakes and learn from them—they are valuable lessons in your journey towards financial mastery.

Incorporating financial education and skill building into your plan is a foundational step towards achieving financial mastery. By empowering yourself with knowledge and expertise, you can make informed decisions, mitigate risks, and seize opportunities to build wealth and secure your future.

In the next chapter, we'll explore the importance of cultivating positive habits and mindsets for financial success. We'll delve into the habits, attitudes, and behaviours that distinguish successful individuals from the rest, and how you can cultivate them to achieve your financial goals with confidence and resilience. Until then, commit to lifelong learning and skill building as essential components of your journey towards financial freedom and remember that knowledge is the key that unlocks the door to a brighter financial future.

Chapter 18
**Cultivating Positive Habits
and Mindsets for Financial Success**

In this chapter, we'll embark on a journey to uncover the essential habits and mindsets that lay the foundation for lasting financial success. The size of your success is measured by the strength of your desire, the size of your dream, and how you handle disappointment along the way.

Understanding the Power of Habits and Mindsets

At the core of every successful financial journey lies a set of positive habits and mindsets that shape attitudes, behaviours, and outcomes. Cultivating these habits and mindsets empowers you to overcome obstacles, seize opportunities, and achieve your financial goals with confidence and resilience.

Let's delve deeper into why habits and mindsets are so crucial:

Discipline: Positive habits such as budgeting, saving, and investing require discipline and consistency to maintain. By cultivating disciplined habits, you develop the self-control and willpower needed to resist temptation, delay gratification, and stay focused on your long-term goals.

Resilience: Financial success is not without its challenges and setbacks. Cultivating a resilient mindset enables you to bounce back from setbacks, learn from failures, and persevere in the face of adversity. Resilience allows you to weather the storms of life with grace and determination, emerging stronger and wiser on the other side.

Growth Mindset: A growth mindset is characterized by a belief in one's ability to learn, grow, and improve over time. Cultivating a growth mindset enables you to embrace challenges, seek feedback, and view failure as an opportunity for growth and development.

With a growth mindset, you approach your financial journey with optimism, curiosity, and a willingness to adapt and evolve.

Abundance Mentality: An abundance mentality is the belief that there is more than enough wealth and opportunity to go around. Cultivating an abundance mentality frees you from scarcity thinking and fosters a sense of gratitude, generosity, and optimism. With an abundance mentality, you approach your financial journey with confidence, creativity, and a willingness to share your wealth and knowledge with others.

Cultivating Positive Habits and Mindsets

Now that we understand the importance of habits and mindsets let's explore how to cultivate them for financial success:

Set Clear Goals: Start by setting clear, specific, and achievable financial goals that align with your values, priorities, and aspirations. Write down your goals, break them down into actionable steps, and commit to pursuing them with unwavering determination and focus.

Develop Daily Rituals: Establish daily rituals and routines that reinforce positive financial habits. Whether it's reviewing your budget, tracking your expenses, or reading financial literature, incorporate activities into your daily routine that support your long-term financial goals and reinforce your commitment to success.

Practice Gratitude: Cultivate an attitude of gratitude for the abundance in your life, both financial and otherwise.

Take time each day to reflect on the blessings, opportunities, and successes you've experienced, and express gratitude for the support, resources, and relationships that contribute to your well-being and happiness.

Embrace Failure: View failure not as a setback, but as a stepping stone on the path to success. Embrace failure as an opportunity for growth, learning, and self-improvement. Reflect on your mistakes, extract valuable lessons from them, and use them to inform your future actions and decisions.

Cultivating positive habits and mindsets is the cornerstone of your journey towards financial success. By developing discipline, resilience, growth mindset, and abundance mentality, you lay the groundwork for achieving your goals and realizing your dreams.

In the next chapter, we'll explore opportunities for passive income and wealth generation. We'll delve into strategies for building multiple streams of income, leveraging assets, and creating financial independence through passive income streams. Until then, commit to cultivating positive habits and mindsets that empower you to achieve your financial goals, and remember that success is not a destination but a journey of growth and self-discovery.

Chapter 19
Exploring Opportunities for Passive Income & Wealth Generation

In this chapter, we'll embark on a journey to explore the myriad possibilities for generating passive income and building wealth that can pave the way to a life of abundance and freedom. The richest people in the world look for and build networks; everyone else looks for work.

Understanding the Power of Passive Income

Passive income is the holy grail of financial success—a steady stream of income that flows into your pocket with minimal ongoing effort or active involvement. Unlike earned income from a job, passive income allows you to leverage your time, money, and resources to generate wealth while you sleep, freeing you from the constraints of traditional employment and empowering you to live life on your own terms.

Let's delve deeper into why passive income is so crucial:

Freedom: Passive income provides financial freedom by decoupling your income from your time. With passive income streams, you're not tied to a 9-to-5 job or trading hours for dollars. Instead, you have the freedom to pursue your passions, spend time with loved ones, and live life on your own terms, knowing that your passive income streams are working for you around the clock.

Scalability: Passive income streams have the potential for scalability and exponential growth. Unlike earned income, which is limited by the number of hours you can work, passive income streams can be scaled up through automation, delegation, and leveraging assets. With the right strategy, you can create multiple streams of passive income that generate increasing returns over time, accelerating your journey towards financial independence.

Stability: Passive income streams provide stability and resilience in the face of economic uncertainty and market volatility. Diversifying your income sources with passive income streams helps mitigate risk and protect against unforeseen setbacks, ensuring a steady flow of income regardless of external factors.

Legacy Building: Passive income streams have the potential to create a lasting legacy for future generations. By building wealth through passive income, you can secure financial security and prosperity not only for yourself but also for your loved ones, heirs, and charitable causes, leaving a lasting impact that extends far beyond your lifetime.

Exploring Opportunities for Passive Income and Wealth Generation

Now that we understand the power of passive income let's explore some of the most popular and effective strategies for generating passive income:

Rental Properties: Real estate investing is one of the most time-tested and reliable ways to generate passive income. By purchasing rental properties, you can earn a steady stream of rental income while building equity and appreciation over time. Whether it's residential or commercial properties, rental real estate offers the potential for long-term wealth accumulation and financial security.

Dividend Stocks: Investing in dividend-paying stocks allows you to earn passive income through regular dividend payments from profitable companies. By building a diversified portfolio of dividend stocks, you can enjoy a reliable stream of income while benefiting from potential capital appreciation over the long term.

Peer-to-Peer Lending: Peer-to-peer lending platforms enable you to earn passive income by lending money to individuals or businesses in exchange for interest payments. By investing in peer-to-peer loans, you can earn attractive returns while diversifying your investment portfolio and spreading risk across multiple borrowers.

Digital Assets: The internet has opened up a world of opportunities for generating passive income through digital assets such as e-books, online courses, membership sites, and digital products. By creating and selling digital assets, you can generate passive income streams that leverage your expertise, creativity, and intellectual property.

Exploring opportunities for passive income and wealth generation is a pivotal step towards achieving financial freedom and abundance. By leveraging passive income streams, you can create a solid foundation of financial security and build wealth that lasts a lifetime.

In the next final chapter, we'll explore the power of setting stretch goals to challenge and expand your financial horizons. We'll delve into strategies for setting ambitious yet achievable goals that push you outside your comfort zone and propel you towards greater levels of success and fulfilment. Until then, explore the opportunities for passive income and wealth generation that resonate with you, and remember that financial freedom is within your reach if you're willing to seize the opportunities that come your way.

Chapter 20

Setting Stretch Goals to Challenge and Expand Your Financial Horizons

In this final chapter, we'll delve into the transformative power of setting stretch goals - audacious objectives that propel you beyond the boundaries of mediocrity and toward unparalleled success. The size of your success is determined by how much of your discomfort zone you're willing to live in.

Understanding the Essence of Stretch Goals

Stretch goals are not mere targets; they are bold declarations of intent that challenge you to reach for the stars and push the limits of what you believe is possible. These audacious aspirations compel you to dream big, think expansively, and embrace a vision of success that transcends conventional boundaries. By stretching your imagination and defying the status quo, you unlock the doors to unlimited potential and chart a course toward financial greatness.

Let's delve deeper into why setting stretch goals is paramount:

Visionary Thinking: Stretch goals ignite the spark of visionary thinking within you, inspiring you to imagine a future that surpasses your wildest dreams. These audacious aspirations compel you to think big, dream boldly, and envision a life of abundance and prosperity that exceeds your current reality. By stretching your imagination, you tap into a wellspring of creativity and innovation that propels you toward greatness.

Unwavering Determination: Setting stretch goals requires unwavering determination and relentless pursuit of excellence. These audacious aspirations demand more than just effort; they demand grit, resilience, and the courage to persevere in the face of adversity. By committing to your stretch goals with unyielding resolve, you harness the power of determination to overcome obstacles, navigate challenges, and achieve extraordinary results.

Accelerated Growth: Stretch goals catalyse accelerated growth and exponential progress, propelling you toward levels of achievement that were once deemed unattainable. By pushing yourself beyond your comfort zone, you unlock hidden reservoirs of potential and cultivate the skills, knowledge, and experience necessary to achieve remarkable results. With each milestone achieved, you elevate your game, expand your horizons, and accelerate your journey toward financial mastery.

Empowerment and Fulfilment: Setting stretch goals empowers you to take control of your financial destiny and create a life of purpose, passion, and fulfilment. These audacious aspirations inspire you to pursue your deepest desires and highest aspirations, unleashing a sense of empowerment and fulfilment that transcends monetary success. By aligning your actions with your stretch goals, you create a roadmap for personal and financial fulfilment that guides you toward lasting happiness and fulfilment.

Setting Stretch Goals

Now that we understand the essence of stretch goals, let's explore how to set them effectively:

Dream Big: Begin by daring to dream big and envisioning the life of abundance and prosperity you desire. Ask yourself: What does financial success look like to me? What are my wildest dreams and aspirations? Dare to dream without limitations and allow yourself to envision a future that surpasses your wildest imagination.

Challenge Conventional Thinking: Challenge conventional thinking and question the limits of what is possible. Refuse to be bound by the constraints of your current circumstances or the expectations of others. Instead, embrace uncertainty as an opportunity for growth, innovation, and exploration. Dare to defy convention and set your sights on achieving the extraordinary.

Set Specific Targets: Define clear, specific, and measurable targets that embody your stretch goals. Break down your audacious aspirations into smaller, actionable steps and milestones that you can track and measure along the way. By setting specific targets, you create a roadmap for success and establish a clear path toward achieving your most ambitious objectives.

Embrace Failure as a Stepping Stone: Embrace failure as an inevitable part of the journey toward greatness. Understand that setbacks and challenges are not signs of defeat but rather opportunities for growth, learning, and self-improvement. Instead of fearing failure, embrace it as a valuable teacher that provides valuable lessons and insights to propel you forward on your path to success.

Incorporating Stretch Goals into Your Financial Plan

Now that you've set your stretch goals, it's time to incorporate them into your financial plan:

Align Your Actions: Align your daily actions and decisions with your stretch goals, ensuring that each choice you make brings you closer to realizing your audacious aspirations. Whether it's saving more, investing strategically, or pursuing new opportunities, ensure that your financial plan reflects your unwavering commitment to achieving greatness.

Stay Flexible and Adapt: Remain flexible and adaptable in the pursuit of your stretch goals, adjusting your strategies and tactics as needed to overcome obstacles and seize opportunities. Remember that the path to success is rarely linear, and it's okay to pivot and course-correct along the way. Stay nimble, stay agile, and stay focused on the prize.

Celebrate Your Progress: Celebrate your progress and milestones along the journey toward your stretch goals. Each step forward is a testament to your courage, determination, and resilience. Take the time to acknowledge your achievements and use them as fuel to propel you toward even greater heights of success.

Setting stretch goals is the ultimate act of courage, vision, and determination - a declaration of your unwavering commitment to greatness and a testament to your belief in your own potential.

Bringing everything into harmony

In this book, "Setting Your Financial Goals: Wealth Strategies," we've embarked on a journey together to unlock the secrets of financial success and we've delved deep into the art of setting and achieving financial goals with purpose and precision.

From defining your vision of financial success to crafting actionable plans to reach your objectives, we've left no stone unturned in our quest for wealth mastery. You've learned how to assess your current financial situation, prioritize your goals, and create a roadmap for success that aligns with your values and aspirations.

But setting financial goals is just the beginning. To truly achieve wealth and abundance, you must also cultivate the mindset and habits of the wealthy. You've discovered the importance of thinking like an investor, embracing calculated risks, and seeking out opportunities for passive income and wealth generation.

Throughout this journey, you've been empowered to take control of your financial destiny, armed with the knowledge and tools you need to succeed. Whether you're aiming to build a comfortable nest egg for retirement, create generational wealth for your family, or pursue your wildest dreams, the strategies outlined in this book will guide you every step of the way.

So, as you close these pages and embark on your own personal journey towards financial freedom, remember this: the path to wealth is not always easy, but it is always worth it. Stay focused on your goals, remain flexible in your approach, and never lose sight of the vision you've created for yourself.

Chapter 1: Defining Your Vision: What Does Financial Success Mean to You?

In this foundational chapter, we explore the importance of establishing a clear vision of financial success. By defining what wealth means to you personally, you lay the groundwork for setting meaningful and achievable goals.

Chapter 2: Assessing Your Current Financial Situation

Before charting a course for the future, it's crucial to understand where you stand financially today. We guide you through a comprehensive assessment of your assets, liabilities, income, and expenses, providing insights that will inform your goal-setting process.

Chapter 3: Identifying Short-Term and Long-Term Goals

Goals serve as the roadmap to your financial destination. In this chapter, we help you identify both short-term and long-term objectives, ensuring that your aspirations are aligned with your vision of financial success.

Chapter 4: Setting Specific, Measurable, Achievable, Relevant, and Time-bound (SMART) Goals

To turn your dreams into reality, it's essential to set goals that are SMART. We break down this acronym and guide you through the process of crafting goals that are specific, measurable, achievable, relevant, and time bound.

Chapter 5: Prioritizing Your Financial Objectives

With a multitude of goals vying for your attention, prioritization is key. We help you evaluate your goals based on their importance, urgency, and impact, enabling you to focus your efforts on what matters most.

Chapter 6: Breaking Down Goals into Actionable Steps

Goals without action are merely wishes. In this chapter, we provide strategies for breaking down your goals into actionable steps, empowering you to make steady progress toward your financial aspirations.

Chapter 7: Creating a Budget to Support Your Goals

A budget is a powerful tool for aligning your spending with your goals. We walk you through the process of creating a budget that supports your financial objectives, helping you allocate resources effectively and efficiently.

Chapter 8: Establishing Emergency Funds and Contingency Plans

Life is unpredictable, but with proper planning, you can weather any storm. We discuss the importance of establishing emergency funds and contingency plans, ensuring that you're prepared for the unexpected.

Chapter 9: Aligning Your Goals with Your Values and Lifestyle

True wealth encompasses more than just financial prosperity; it's about living a life aligned with your values and priorities. We guide you in aligning your financial goals with your core values and desired lifestyle, fostering a sense of fulfilment and purpose.

Chapter 10: Overcoming Common Obstacles to Goal Setting

Along the journey to financial success, you're likely to encounter obstacles and challenges. We explore common barriers to goal setting and provide strategies for overcoming them, empowering you to stay on track and persevere in the face of adversity.

Chapter 11: Staying Motivated and Persistent Throughout the Process

Maintaining motivation and persistence is essential for achieving long-term success. We offer techniques for staying motivated and focused on your goals, ensuring that you remain committed to your financial journey even when the going gets tough.

Chapter 12: Celebrating Milestones and Progress Along the Way

Celebrating your achievements, no matter how small, is crucial for maintaining momentum and morale. We encourage you to acknowledge and celebrate milestones along your financial journey, recognizing the progress you've made and fuelling your determination to continue moving forward.

Chapter 13: Reviewing and Adjusting Goals as Needed

Flexibility is key to successful goal setting. In this chapter, we discuss the importance of regularly reviewing and adjusting your goals based on changing circumstances and priorities, ensuring that your financial plan remains relevant and effective.

Chapter 14: Seeking Professional Advice and Guidance

Building wealth is a complex endeavour, and seeking professional advice can provide valuable insights and expertise. We explore the benefits of working with financial advisors, accountants, and other professionals to optimize your financial strategy and maximize your success.

Chapter 15: Leveraging Technology and Tools to Track Your Progress

In today's digital age, a wealth of technology and tools are available to help you track and manage your finances. We highlight some of the most useful resources and discuss how you can leverage them to monitor your progress and stay on course toward your goals.

Chapter 16: Surrounding Yourself with a Supportive Network

Surrounding yourself with a supportive network of friends, family, and mentors can provide invaluable encouragement and guidance on your financial journey. We discuss the importance of building a strong support system and offer tips for cultivating positive relationships that foster your growth and success.

Chapter 17: Incorporating Financial Education and Skill Building into Your Plan

Continuous learning and skill development are essential components of financial success. We explore the importance of financial education and offer recommendations for expanding your knowledge and expertise in areas such as investing, budgeting, and wealth management.

Chapter 18: Cultivating Positive Habits and Mindsets for Financial Success

Your habits and mindset play a significant role in shaping your financial outcomes. We delve into the habits and mindsets of successful wealth builders, providing insights and strategies for cultivating positive behaviours that support your journey toward financial success.

Chapter 19: Exploring Opportunities for Passive Income and Wealth Generation

Passive income streams can provide a valuable supplement to your primary income and accelerate your path to wealth. We explore various opportunities for generating passive income, from real estate investing to online business ventures, and offer guidance on how to capitalize on these opportunities effectively.

Chapter 20: Setting Stretch Goals to Challenge and Expand Your Financial Horizons

As you progress on your financial journey, it's essential to continue challenging yourself and striving for greater heights of success. We discuss the concept of stretch goals and offer strategies for setting ambitious yet attainable objectives that push you outside your comfort zone and propel you toward ever-greater levels of wealth and abundance.

Conclusion

In "Setting Your Financial Goals: Wealth Strategies," we've covered a wealth of knowledge and practical strategies for achieving financial success. From defining your vision of wealth to crafting actionable plans and overcoming obstacles along the way, you now possess the tools and insights you need to build the financial future of your dreams. Remember, wealth is not just about money - it's about living a life of purpose, fulfilment, and abundance. So go forth with confidence, dear reader, and may your journey be filled with prosperity, joy, and endless possibilities.